WELCOME

—

Girl, You Got This, is an eBook created by Bluhazl, four women who dream to inspire you to live your best life holistically, physically and mentally. BluHazl is a space for women to connect and embrace sisterhood because we believe that we are all sisters here. Sharing our passions through nutritional recipes, health + wellness, and empowerment has created a community of strong and committed women who want to live their best life surrounded by powerful and supportive women.

GIRL, YOU GOT THIS!

D'ANA ROLLE

[NUTRITIONAL RECIPES]

@BLUHAZL

I love creating quick, nutritional, and tasteful dishes by using minimal ingredients. I believe in nutrition and knowing exactly what I am putting into my body. You've got to glow from the inside, out.

LATICIA ROLLE

[QUOTES AND SISTERHOOD]

@BLUHAZL

Empowered women, empower women.
I believe in the power of sisterhood and in women supporting women. I believe in loving your tribe endlessly and the importance of loving yourself even harder. Something special happens when strong women come together. Be the light.

CODIE CABRAL

[DO IT YOURSELF]

@CODIECABRAL

My mission in life is not merely to survive, but to thrive. Once I realized that a healthy outside starts with a healthy inside, my life was changed forever. Fall in love with taking care of your body, it's the only one you have. Keep it clean, keep it green, and keep it minimal.

LAUREN WILLIAMS

[FITNESS]

@LAJOY224

Fitness is a gateway to a healthy body, mind and soul believe that the benefits you get from training reach far beyond the physical. Time spent training is time investing in the best version of yourself.

Stop comparing
yourself to others.
You have everything
you need inside of you.
Dig deep and
find your light.
Shine baby, shine.

DEAR SISTER,

Having a shoulder to lean on, an ear to cry to, or someone to call when you have pure joy to spill is priceless. That's why we have our sisterhood tribe to turn to whenever we need them. Side by side, or miles apart, we are all sisters connected by the heart.

Laticia

DEAR SISTER,

Do you know how beautiful you are? I mean, do you know how stunning you truly are and how bright your soul shines? I know it's tough to see some days, but let me be the first to tell you, YOU ARE BEAUTIFUL. Girl, you are special and you are the only person that can make yourself think otherwise. Let that sink in; it's all in your mind.

Remember, we are all given special qualities that make us different, embrace your badass traits that separate you from the rest. Find these qualities and shine baby, shine! When that inner beauty blooms, a flower is born. Be that flower, and grow amongst the other beautiful flowers. You are beautiful. Never let anyone or anything dim your shine.

You might be wondering, "but how do I find my shine?" Girl, find it within yourself first! Dig deep, discover yourself, embrace your differences, love yourself, and accept your flaws. Understand that perfection does not exist and that you will have highs and lows, but your perspective is everything. Create a mindset to see the good in everything. Control your destiny. Each morning you have a chance to wake up and be thankful. Continue to live your best life. Believe in your magic, sister.

YOU ARE BEAUTIFUL.

DEAR SISTER

My mother often said, "You are the people you surround yourself with." The older I become, the more I understand the truth of my mother's wise words. Surrounding yourself with people who challenge and inspire you will make you ten times the woman you are now. Finding a tribe that uplifts and supports you will change your life. Look around you, is your tribe making you better?

Your tribe may change as you grow and that's fine. Not everyone will always be on the same wavelength as you. Find your tribe and love your tribe. Accept the challenge that your sisterhood presents to you, for they will always have your best interest. These fascinating people are the people you never want to let go. Observe how much you bloom when everyone waters you with inspiration and encouragement. Cherish sisterhood and it will change your life.

FIND YOUR TRIBE

Dear Sister

Like any relationship, being a part of a sisterhood takes work and dedication. Once you find your tribe understand how fortunate you are to experience this unbreakable bond of sisterhood.

THE 5 RULES OF SISTERHOOD:

1. Be her #1 fan.

Always and forever, I'll root for my sister no matter what. My sister is an extension of me. When she wins, I win.

2. Always listen.

Even when you don't want to listen to the same story over and OVER again, just be patient. Your sister needs you the most. Sit, be kind, and listen.

3. Forgive her.

Forgiveness is the key to sisterhood. We fight, we argue, we may even pull hair, but saying sorry and accepting her apology will make life so much easier. Forgiveness is vital.

4. Tell her when she's wrong.

You have got to be honest with you sister, 24/7, no matter what. Have her back. Be her right hand. Especially if she's wrong, she deserves genuine advice.

5. Help her get it right!

Always be there to pick your sister up, dust her off, and tell her to try again. You are her #1 fan after all, so let her know and never let her give up! Have her back forever and if she falls, help her dust her shoulders off and encourage her to try again. #SISTERPOWER

For more ways to be a better sister, head over to BluHazl.com.

DEAR SISTER,

I know things get tough and you feel like giving up, but in the words of 2 Pac: "you got to keep ya head up." In this journey of life, we all face super highs and crazy lows. We will have amazing days and days when we won't feel like getting out of bed. Guess what, each and everyone us go through days like these. You are not alone, and you are not defined by your struggles. As Diane Von Furstenberg once said: "I never met a woman who wasn't strong." So have faith and believe in yourself.

You are stronger than you think. Get out of your head and know that there is light at the end of the tunnel. The sun will shine tomorrow and carry you into the night, where you will shine amongst the stars. Dust yourself off, talk through your emotions with your tribe and seek help if needed. You are the only one stopping you from bouncing back. Believe, have courage, and know your worth. Girl, we got this.

BOUNCE BACK.

A positive mind will create a positive life.

3 WAYS TO STAY POSITIVE:

Write down positive and motivational quotes and place them all around you!

Personally, I always grab an old lipstick and write positive quotes on every mirror in my house. Sticky notes work too! Write down what you want or what you would like the universe to send you. I totally suggest you write as many quotes, words, affirmations and dreams down and place them all around you so you're constantly providing yourself positive vibes. TRUST ME, the more positivity you see, the more your life will be surrounded by positivity.

A Daily Mantra!

"I am strong. I am confident. I am successful." This mantra allows me to remind myself WHO I AM, because some days when I feel out of it, I can't allow myself to get lost in the dark. Affirmations are powerful tools to allow yourself to be open to accepting all the greatness you deserve. Never forget WHO YOU ARE, WHERE YOU ARE GOING, and WHAT YOU WANT! Give yourself a daily mantra to help guide you throughout your day to day life.

Breathe.

If you're anything like me, some days you may forget to just slow down and BREATHE. Be patient, relax and BREATHE. Take a couple minutes of your day to yourself, find a quiet place and just breathe. Blow the anxiety or stress away.

Girl, we got this.

POSITIVITY.

EAT GOOD.
FEEL GOOD.
LOOK GOOD.
LIVE GOOD.

NUTRITION

An individual's thoughts on food can be skewed so quickly—my role is to connect and empower women by sharing helpful tips, recipes, knowledge, and love for nutrition. I believe that we're all on a ride to vibrate higher. I believe that food is medicine. I believe that real food matters. I believe in moderation. I believe that cooking with minimal ingredients to create quick, flavorful, and fun recipes is key.

D'Ana

ALL INGREDIENTS ARE ENCOURAGED TO BE *ORGANIC
ALL RECIPES ARE MADE WITH REAL FOOD
ALL RECIPES ARE TAILORED TO PROMOTE BODY BEAUTY
ALL RECIPES ARE TAILORED TO BE A MORNING (OR SNACK) BOOST

HAZL'S RECIPE REFERENCE

A FEW FACT-FILLED NOTES ON WHY THESE RECIPES ARE GOOD FOR YA!
CHECK THE CORRESPONDING RECIPE NUMBER FOR THE DEETS.

1.

Greens, greens, greens—the new breakfast craze. Starting your morning off with a green smoothie packed with vitamins, minerals, fiber, antioxidants, and polyphenols is the perfect way to stimulate digestion, metabolism, and rid your body of toxins. Don't be intimidated by the greens; have fun and try something new!

2.

You bes' believe the hype about matcha, because it's the real deal! Matcha is powdered green tea leaves—it's that simple—but by using the leaves instead of just steeping them in water, you're getting amplified health benefits from the green tea. Matcha detoxifies the body with its high levels of chlorophyll, prevents cancer-causing cells thanks to its naturally occurring compound called catechins, and on top of that, it's packed with antioxidants to promote energy, weight loss, and brain power. #WINNING

3.

I live for a powerhouse smoothie that contains multiple functional foods. Cacao is packed with high-levels of magnesium, an abundant amount of antioxidants, as well as being a natural mood booster and anti-depressant. Turmeric is a spice I cannot live without, as it inhibits cancer cell-growth, boosts the cardiovascular system, and is a major anti-inflammatory. Give your energy a boost with the power of collagen whey, and make yourself a CTP smoothie to conquer the day!

4.

Did you know that gut health is linked to our overall wellbeing? For example, up to 80 percent of our immune system lives in our gut, which is one of the many reasons our gut is considered to be our "second" brain. If poor digestion is cramping your style, you're not alone—girl, we got this! Cheers to gut-loving smoothies.

5.

Do you ever find yourself stressed out and running out of options to soothe your nerves? YES—me too. Daily. Don't fret. Allow me to introduce you to adaptogens. This is a unique class of healing plants that help balance, restore, and protect the body. Girl, let's get our cortisol levels and adrenal glands in-check the all-natural way before we age ourselves too quickly!

6.

I will be a fan of peanut butta' and jelly foreverever. But this time around, I'mtransforming my PB&J into overnight oats with one of my favorite mushroom adaptogens: reishi. Reishi will help regulate cellular functions and promote calmness,centeredness, balance, inner awareness, and inner strength. #REISHI4PRESIDENT

7.

Waffles for breakfast? Everyday? #YASGIRL. I'm sharing my favorite waffle recipe with you and yo' girls as it's packed with proteins and fiber that will help improve digestion and show extra loving to your heart.

8.

Did you know that utilizing sprouted grains enables the activation of dormant nutrients during the sprouting process? More protein, more vitamins, and more minerals—sign me up. #THANKMELATER. Don't forget to add in a scoop of Vital Proteins collagen whey to improve overall athletic performance and recovery!

9.

Have you realized yet that I sneak in teaspoons of superfoods in just about every recipe? Cheers to body loving stuffed french toast skewers packed with powerful antioxidants and gut-loving easily digestible sprouted bread!

10.

I'm kicking McDonald's egg-McMuffins to the curb and creating flavor-packed egg muffins for everyday eats packed with real ingredients. Don't feel intimidated by the ingredient list—add or take away whatever you choose!

Bring On The Greens Smoothie

INGREDIENTS—MAKES 1 SERVING

1 HANDFUL KALE
1 HANDFUL ROMAINE
¼ CUP PARSLEY, FRESH
¼ CUP CILANTRO, FRESH
½ GREEN APPLE, ROUGH CHOP
½ CUP PINEAPPLE, FROZEN
2 STALKS CELERY
½ CUCUMBER, ROUGH CHOP
½-INCH KNOB GINGER, FRESH, PEELED, SLICED
½ TEASPOON CAYENNE
1 LEMON, JUICED
2 CUPS COCONUT WATER

Using a high-speed blender, add all ingredients in order starting from top to bottom.

Blend on medium speed for 30-45 seconds or until silky smooth.

You may add more liquid to achieve desired consistency.

Pour into preferred glass and serve with desired toppings—such as yogurt, granola, hemp hearts, bee pollen or peanut butter.

Serve immediately.

Avo-Matcha Smoothie Bowl

INGREDIENTS—MAKES 1 SERVING

- 2 CUPS SPINACH
- 1 AVOCADO
- 1 CUP MANGO, FROZEN
- ½ CUP CAULIFLOWER, FROZEN
- 4 MEDJOOL DATES, PITTED
- 2 TEASPOONS MATCHA POWDER
- 1 SCOOP VITAL PROTEINS COLLAGEN PEPTIDES
- 1 LEMON, JUICED
- 2 CUPS NON-DAIRY MILK

Using a high-speed blender, add all ingredients in order starting from top to bottom.

Blend on medium speed for 30-45 seconds or until silky smooth. You may add more liquid to achieve desired consistency.

Pour into preferred bowl and serve with desired toppings—such as yogurt, granola, goji berries, coconut flakes, raisins or fresh mango.

Serve immediately.

Cacao Turmeric Protein Smoothie

INGREDIENTS—MAKES 1 SERVING

1 HANDFUL KALE
¼ CUP COCONUT MEAT, FROZEN
2 BANANAS, FROZEN
3-4 MEDJOOL DATES, PITTED
½-INCH KNOB TURMERIC, FRESH, PEELED, SLICED
1 TEASPOON CACAO POWDER
1 SCOOP VITAL PROTEINS COCOA-COCONUT COLLAGEN WHEY
1 TEASPOON MATCHA POWDER
2 CUPS NON-DAIRY MILK

Using a high-speed blender, add all ingredients in order starting from top to bottom.

Blend on medium speed for 30-45 seconds or until silky smooth.

You may add more liquid to achieve desired consistency.

Pour into preferred bowl and serve with desired toppings—such as yogurt, granola, goji berries, coconut flakes, raisins or fresh mango.

Serve immediately.

Digestion Enhancing Smoothie

INGREDIENTS—MAKES 1 SERVING

1 HANDFUL KALE
¼ CUP PARSLEY
¼ CUP MINT, FRESH
½ CUP PINEAPPLE, FROZEN
½ AVOCADO
½-INCH KNOB GINGER, FRESH, PEELED, SLICED
1 BANANA, FROZEN
¼ TEASPOON PROBIOTIC POWDER
1 LEMON, JUICED
2 CUP NON-DAIRY MILK

Using a high-speed blender, add all ingredients in order starting from top to bottom.

Blend on medium speed for 30-45 seconds or until silky smooth. You may add more liquid to achieve desired consistency.

Pour into preferred bowl and serve with desired toppings—such as yogurt, granola, dried cherries, coconut flakes or fresh fruits.

Serve immediately.

Boost That Mood A-Latte

INGREDIENTS—MAKES 1 SERVING

2 CUPS NON-DAIRY MILK, WARMED
2 MEDJOOL DATES, PITTED
1 TEASPOON VANILLA BEAN GHEE
2 TEASPOONS MATCHA
½ TEASPOON CINNAMON
1 TEASPOON MACA
½ TEASPOON ASHWAGANDAHA
½ TEASPOON TOCOS
½ TEASPOON HE SHOU WU
1 SCOOP VITAL PROTEINS COLLAGEN PEPTIDES

In a small saucepot over medium heat, warm non-dairy milk just before it begins to boil for ~ 4-5 minutes.

Using a high-speed blender, add all ingredients in order starting from top to bottom.

Blend on medium speed for 30 seconds or until silky smooth and frothy.

Serve immediately.

Peanut Butter-Banana & J Overnight Oats

INGREDIENTS—MAKES 1 SERVING

FOR OATS
½ CUP SPROUTED OATS, GLUTEN-FREE
1 ¼ CUP NON-DAIRY MILK
1 RIPE BANANA, MASHED
1 TEASPOON REISHI
4 TABLESPOONS PEANUT BUTTER
FOR BERRY CHIA JAM
½ CUP RASPBERRIES, FROZEN
½ CUP STRAWBERRIES, FROZEN
2 TABLESPOONS CHIA SEEDS
1 TEASPOON VANILLA

The night before
Prepare oats. In a mason jar (or container of choice) combine oats, milk, and banana. Stir to mix. Cover mason jar and shake for 30 seconds to combine. Leave in refrigerator overnight.

Prepare berry chia jam. In a small saucepan over medium heat, add berries and allow to cook until fragrant for ~2-3 minutes. Using a fork, mash the berries leaving a few chunks. Reduce heat to low, add chia seeds and vanilla. Allow mixture to simmer for ~5 minutes. Remove from heat. Store in airtight container overnight to allow for jam to thicken.

The morning of
Remove oats and jam from refrigerator. Add ½ cup of berry chia jam to oats jar and swirl in peanut butter. Serve with desired toppings—such as granola, hemp seeds, goji berries, or fresh berries for example.

Store leftovers in airtight container in the refrigerator for up to 2 days.

Choco-nana Protein Waffles

INGREDIENTS—MAKES 10-12 WAFFLES

1 CUP SPROUTED OAT FLOUR
¼ CUP ALMOND FLOUR
½ CUP BUCKWHEAT FLOUR
2 TEASPOONS BAKING POWDER
1 TEASPOON BAKING SODA
2 TEASPOON CINNAMON
1 TEASPOON MATCHA POWDER
2 TEASPOONS CACAO POWDER
1 PASTURE-RAISED EGG
3 RIPE BANANA, MASHED
2 TABLESPOON CHIA SEEDS
1 TEASPOON VANILLA
1 TABLESPOON MAPLE SYRUP
1 CUP NON-DAIRY MILK
1 TABLESPOON COCONUT OIL, MELTED

In a large mixing bowl, whisk together oat flour, almond flour, buckwheat flour, baking powder, baking powder, cinnamon, matcha and cacao powder. Set aside.

In another large mixing bowl, whisk together egg, mashed banana, chia seeds, vanilla, maple syrup, non-dairy milk, and melted coconut oil. Mix until combined. Add wet ingredients into above dry ingredients.

Heat waffle iron to medium heat setting. Coat with coconut oil.

(If you want to keep waffles warm before serving, preheat oven to 200 degrees F and place a baking sheet tray lined with parchment inside.)

Pour ½ cup of batter into a coconut oil greased waffle iron. Let cook until golden brown. Remove from iron. Transfer waffles to warming sheet tray while you finish cooking the remainder of the waffle batter.

Serve with desired toppings—such as granola, yogurt, fresh banana, fresh berries, toasted almonds or peanut butter.

Store any leftovers in an airtight container in the refrigerator for up to 3 days.

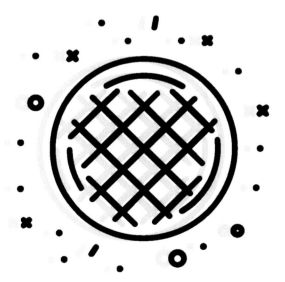

Mini-Granola Bowls

INGREDIENTS—MAKES 10 CUPCAKE SIZED BOWLS

FOR DRY INGREDIENTS
2 CUPS SPROUTED OATS, GLUTEN-FREE
4 TABLESPOONS COCONUT FLOUR
2 TEASPOONS CINNAMON
1 TEASPOON MATCHA
1 SCOOP VITAL PROTEINS VANILLA COCONUT COLLAGEN WHEY
½ CUP DRIED CHERRIES

FOR WET INGREDIENTS
1 FLAX-EGG (1 TABLESPOON FLAX MEAL + 3 TABLESPOONS WARM WATER)
¼ CUP COCONUT OIL, MELTED
¼ CUP MAPLE SYRUP
5 TABLESPOONS ALMOND BUTTER, MELTED

Preheat oven to 350 degrees F. Line cupcake tray with liners. Set aside.

Make flax-egg: combine flax meal and water in a small bowl. Let sit for ~5 minutes or until coagulated.

Sift dry ingredients together into a medium-sized mixing bowl.

Combine wet ingredients into a small mixing bowl. Add flax-egg. Whisk until fully incorporated.

Add wet ingredients to dry ingredients. Mix until combined.

Fill each cupcake liner ½ way full and lightly press the mixture forming a mini-bowl pushing up high on the sides to create the bowl walls.

Bake in oven for 15-20 minutes. Bowls should be fragrant and golden brown. Remove from oven, let cool, and serve with desired toppings—such as yogurt, granola, fresh fruits, coconut flakes, cacao nibs, or peanut butter.

Store any leftovers in an airtight container in the refrigerator for up to 5 days.

Stuffed French Toast Skewers

INGREDIENTS—MAKES 4 SKEWERS

FOR BREAD
3 RIPE BANANAS, MASHED
½ AVOCADO, PITTED, MASHED
1 TABLESPOON CACAO POWDER
1 TEASPOON MATCHA POWDER
2 TABLESPOON MAPLE SYRUP
1 TEASPOON VANILLA
4 SLICES OF SPROUTED EZEKIEL BREAD

FOR EGG WASH
2 EGGS
3 TEASPOONS CINNAMON
1 TEASPOON VANILLA
1 TABLESPOON COCONUT OIL, MELTED
1 CUP NON-DAIRY MILK

FOR SKEWERS
16 ½-INCH DICED PINEAPPLES, GRILLED
4 SKEWERS

In a small mixing bowl, combine mashed bananas, avocado, cacao powder, matcha powder, maple syrup and vanilla. Mix until combined.

Place two slices of bread on a cutting board. Spread above mixture evenly on both slices and top with the remaining two slices.

Make egg wash: combine all ingredients in a medium bowl and whisk until incorporated. Set aside.

Grease a 10-inch cast iron skillet with coconut oil and warm up over medium heat. Dredge each stuffed sandwich, one at time, in the egg wash. Place each sandwich on preheated cast iron skillet. Cook for ~5 minutes on each side or until fragrant and golden brown.

In the meantime, using a stove top grill pan over medium heat, coat with coconut oil and grill each piece of pineapple for ~5 minutes. Turn off heat. Set aside.

Remove sandwiches from skillet and place on cutting board. Using a serrated knife, cut each sandwich into 1-inch strips lengthwise and then cut the strips crosswise into 1-inch cubes. Assemble each skewer alternating pineapple and sandwich cubes.

Store any leftovers in an airtight container in the refrigerator for up to 2 days.

Spicy Egg Muffins

INGREDIENTS—MAKES 12 MUFFINS

FOR EGGS

10 EGGS
½ CUP NON-DAIRY MILK
1 HANDFUL KALE, ROUGHLY CHOPPED
½ CUP RED ONION, FINELY DICED
½ CUP GREEN PEPPER, FINELY DICED
¼ CUP SUNDRIED TOMATOES
¼ CUP MUSHROOMS, FINELY DICED
½ CUP CHICKEN SAUSAGE, FINELY DICED

FOR SEASONINGS

1 TABLESPOON CHILI POWDER
1 TABLESPOON RED PEPPER FLAKES
1 TABLESPOON GARLIC POWDER
1 TEASPOON TURMERIC
1 TEASPOON SALT
1 TEASPOON BLACK PEPPER

Preheat oven to 350 degrees F. Spray muffin tin with avocado oil. Set aside.

In a large mixing bowl, whisk together eggs and non-dairy milk.

Add in remaining ingredients and spices. Whisk to combine.

Pour egg batter into muffin tin filling each cup ¾ full.

Bake in oven for 15 minutes or until fluffy and slightly golden on top.

Store leftovers in airtight container in refrigerator for up to 5 days.

> Fitness starts with believing in yourself. Believe you can go the distance and YOU WILL. 99

FITNESS

Our bodies are capable of incredible things, it is our minds that need convincing. Remember to set goals to keep you focused and always celebrate when you reach them! It's also essential to find your workout tribe or fit squad to help you to stay motivated.

Here are 10 workouts to add to your fitness journey.

Girl, You Got This!

Lauren

CHISEL CLUB WORKOUT: RISE & GRIND

Wake up, workout, boss out, repeat. This workout is designed with those tough early mornings in mind. It's perfect for when you need some weighted exercises to get the blood pumping to start your day off right.

Goal: 3-5 rounds / Time: 20 min / Intensity: Moderate

1. RISE & KICK

- **A** - Start in a half kneeling position with one knee on the ground and the opposite foot planted on the ground. Hold weights by the shoulders with elbows pointing down.
- **B** - Stand up on planted foot and kick opposite leg straight ahead. Return to start. That was one rep; do 12 - 15 on each side.

2. RENEGADE ROW

- **A** - Start in standard plank position with a weight in each hand. Your feet are hip width apart or slightly wider. Bend your right elbow raising the weight towards your rib cage, while keeping the rest of your body locked in a plank. Return to start.
- **B** - Repeat on opposite side. That's one rep; do 12 - 15.

3. KNEELING OVERHEAD PRESS

- **A** - Kneel with right knee on the ground and left foot planted flat on the ground. Hold a weight in your left hand by your shoulder.
- **B** - Press weight overhead, aligning bicep by the ear and tightening core. Return to start. That was one rep; do 12 - 15 on each side.

4. DUMBBELL FRONT SQUAT

- **A** - Rise up into a standing position, holding weights at your shoulders, palms facing each other, elbows bent and feet hip width or slightly wider.
- **B** - Lower into a squat, bringing thighs parallel to the ground. Return to start. That is one rep; do 12 - 15.

5. FRONT SHOULDER RAISES

- **A** - Stand tall with feet hip width apart and weight by your side.
- **B** - Squeeze core and butt as you lift weights straight ahead until arms are parallel to the ground. Return to start. That is one rep; do 12 - 15.

chiselclub.com
photographs and graphic design by Fredy Soberanis (soberanisproductions.com)

CHISEL CLUB WORKOUT: THREE DIMENSIONAL

When we workout, it is important to train our bodies to be strong in different planes of motions. This means training our bodies to be strong when we are moving forwards and backwards, side to side or rotating. This workout is designed to add some dImension to your movement patterns.

Goal: 3-5 rounds / Time: 15 min / Intensity: High

1. SIDE LUNGE WITH PUNCH

A - Start standing with feet together, step right foot wide and lower into a side lunge and bend elbows bringing weights up to shoulders. Right leg should be parallel to the ground.
B - Hold lunge and punch left arm forward. Return to start. That is one rep; do 12 - 15 on each side.

2. SIDE TO SIDE SLAMS

A - Hold med ball overhead. Rotate your body to the left as if you are on about a 45 degree angle.
B - Use force from arms, core and legs to slam the ball into the ground. Return to start and repeat on the other side. That is one rep; do 12 - 15.

3. BENTOVER TRICEP KICKBACKS

A - Hinge forward from your hips, slight bend in your knees. Pull weights towards your rib cage, elbows close to your side and pointing to the ceiling.
B - Keep elbows by your side and extend weights behind you, lengthening your arms. Return to start. That is one rep; do 12 - 15.

4. MED BALL CHOPS

A - Start with feet hip width apart in a squat. Rotate hips and torso to the right side. Twist as you bring the med ball to the outside of your right hip.
B - Stand up and rotate to your opposite side, bringing med ball over the left shoulder. Return to start. That is one rep; do 12 - 15 on each side.

5. MED BALL PLANK SWITCH

A - Start in a plank position with hands on the med ball. Plant right foot outside the right hand. Keep left leg straight.
B - Switch, jumping right foot back and bringing left foot up outside the left hand.

chiselclub.com
photographs and graphic design by Fredy Soberanis (soberanisproductions.com)

CHISEL CLUB WORKOUT: MED BALL MADNESS

One tool, five moves. When it's busy at the gym and you are fighting for space and equipment, this workout is perfect. All you need is a med ball to work your entire body. To make it more challenging go for a heavy ball and to dial it back, you can choose a lighter one.

Goal: 3-5 rounds / Time: 25 min / Intensity: Moderate

1. KNEELING ARM RAISE CIRCLES

- **A** - Start kneeling on both knees, toes tucked under. Hold med ball at your chest. Extend ball straight forward, arms are parallel with the ground.
- **B** - Raise ball overhead. Return to start. That is one rep; do 12 - 15.

2. REVERSE LUNGE WITH EXTENDED ARMS

- **A** - Start standing with feet together, holding med ball at your chest. Bring right foot behind you lowering into a lunge.
- **B** - Extend med ball straight in front of you, bringing arms parallel to the ground. Return to start, legs together and med ball at chest. That's one rep; do 12 - 15 on each side.

3. GET UP CRUNCH

- **A** - Lay on back with right leg bent, right foot on the ground. Extend left leg and left arm straight, both at a 45 degree angle from the body. Place med ball in right hand and press the ball to the ceiling extending right arm.
- **B** - Keeping right arm straight and looking at the ball the whole time, peel torso off the ground until shoulders are stacked over left elbow. Return to start. That's one rep; do 10 on each side.

4. BRIDGE TRICEP EXTENSION

- **A** - Start on back, knees bent and feet on the ground. Press med ball with both hands straight to the ceiling.
- **B** - Press hips to the ceiling and reach med ball overhead, hovering just above the ground. Bring med ball in front of chest and hips to starting position. That's one rep; do 12 - 15.

5. RUSSIAN TWISTS

- **A** - In a seated position on the floor, balance on your tailbone and raise legs with bent knees and calves parallel to the ground. Keep chest lifted and med ball in front of your chest. Avoid hunching shoulders and/or rounding back.
- **B** - Rotate torso, bringing med ball to your left side. Then rotate back through center, then to the right side. That's one rep; do 20.

chiselclub.com
photographs and graphic design by Fredy Soberanis (soberanisproductions.com)

CHISEL CLUB WORKOUT: JACK ATTACK

This workout combines some heart pumping jumps and strength moves. Every round starts with jack tucks, which will make the strength moves more challenging to perform. Once you master this workout, you can add in extra jack tucks after each strength move.

Goal: 3-5 rounds / Time: 20 min / Intensity: High

1. JACK TUCKS

- A - Start standing with feet together and arms by your side. Do a jumping jack, bringing arms overhead and feet wider than hips.
- B - Jump feet back together then do a tuck jump: jumping as high as you can and bringing knees in towards the chest. That is one rep; do 20.

2. SINGLE LEG DEADLIFT

- A - Stand straight and shift body weight on left leg. Hold a weight in right hand.
- B - Hinge forward bringing right leg off the ground and bringing weight towards the calf. Keep back straight and shoulder blades pulled together. That is one rep; do 12 - 15 on each side.

3. FLOOR CHEST PRESS

- A - Lay on your back, knees bent and feet planted on the ground. Hold weights in both hands. Elbows are on a 45 degree angled away from torso, palms face your legs.
- B - Press dumbbells towards the ceiling. Stack weights over shoulders. Return to start. That is one rep; do 12 - 15.

4. BENT OVER FLYS

- A - Hinge forward from your hips, slight bend in your knees. Weights hanging in front of you with palms facing each other.
- B - Lead with elbows as your arms reach towards ceiling, squeezing shoulder blades together. Return to start. That is one rep; do 12 - 15.

5. CURL TO OVERHEAD PRESS

- A - Stand tall with feet underneath hips and weights by your side. Core is engaged the whole time.
- B - Curl weights to your shoulders, palms facing towards to you.
- C - Press weight overhead, palms facing you. Lower slowly and return to start. That is one rep; do 12 - 15.

chiselclub.com
photographs and graphic design by Fredy Soberanis (soberanisproductions.com)

CHISEL CLUB WORKOUT: ONLY THE STRONG

To achieve any goal in life, physical or otherwise, you need strength. And strength isn't built overnight, it takes time, persistence and dedication. When you do this workout, push your limits and grab those heavier weights. Yes, the ones you most often shy away from. When you push your limits, you may surprise yourself. You will develop your mental and physical strength in the process. Let's get it.

Goal: 3-5 rounds / Time: 25 min / Intensity: High

1. STAGGERED STANCE DEADLIFT
- **A** - Stand with right foot slightly in front of left. Place most of your weight on the front foot. A weight in each hand at arm's length and by your side.
- **B** - Hinge forward, keeping your body weight on right foot, with a slight bend in the knee. Bring the weights to shins while keeping your back straight. Return to start. That is one rep; do 12 - 15.

2. ALTERNATING ROWS
- **A** - Hinge forward from the hips with a weight in each hand. Your feet are hip width apart. Bend your right elbow raising the weight towards your rib cage. Return to start.
- **B** - Repeat on opposite side. That's one rep; do 12 - 15.

3. LOADED JUMPING LUNGES
- **A** - Start by lowering into a lunge, both knees forming 90 degree angles and weights by your side.
- **B** - Explode off the ground and land back into a lunge, keeping the same leg forward. That is one rep; do 12 - 15 on each side.

4. PLANK JACKS
- **A** - Start in a plank position. Shoulders stacked over wrists and feet touching.
- **B** - Jump feet wider than hip width. Return to start. That is one rep; do 20.

5. SINGLE LEG BRIDGE
- **A** - Lay on back with left leg bent and left foot on the ground. Extend right leg toward ceiling.
- **B** - Press into left foot and press hips to the ceiling. Return to start. That is one rep; do 12 - 15 on each side.

chiselclub.com
photographs and graphic design by Fredy Soberanis (soberanisproductions.com)

CHISEL CLUB WORKOUT: ENDORPHIN BURST

Working out is amazing for your physical health and it is also good for your mental and emotional health. When you workout your body releases endorphins, which trigger a positive feeling in the body. If you are having a hard day, feeling anxious or sad, think about getting a workout in to help you reset your mind and body. This quick HIIT (High Intensity Interval Training) workout is designed to help you get your cardio and your good vibes up!

Goal: 3-5 rounds / Time: 25 min / Intensity: High

1. MOUNTAIN CLIMBERS

- A - Start in a plank position. Shoulders stacked over wrists and feet hip width apart. Bring your right knee in towards your chest while keeping the left leg straight.
- B - Switch, bringing left knee into the chest and right leg out straight at the same time. Keep core core engaged and hips stable. That is one rep; do 20 - 30.

2. 180 SQUAT JUMPS

- A - Lower into a squat position. Jump up out of this position rotating 180 degrees to your left while in the air.
- B - Land in a squat facing the opposite direction. That is one rep; do 20.

3. PUSH UP (HOLD)

- A - Start in a pushup position. Lower down until you are hovering just above the ground.
- B - Hold for 10 secs. Return to start position. That is one rep; do as many as possible!

4. PLYO LUNGES

- A - Start in a lunge position with left leg in front and right leg behind.
- B - Jump and switch legs landing with right leg in front and left leg behind. That is one rep; do 20.

5. CRAB DIPS

- A - Sit on the floor with knees bent, fingers pointing towards you and feet flat on the ground. Lift hips off the ground.
- B - Bend elbows lowering body towards the ground. Then straighten arms to start position. That is one rep; do 12 - 15.

chiselclub.com
photographs and graphic design by Fredy Soberanis (soberanisproductions.com)

CHISEL CLUB WORKOUT: LEVEL UP

Want to take your bodyweight workout up a notch without adding equipment? Try adding levels to it! In this workout, we are going to elevate your push-up, your lunges, your squat jumps and more. This one is perfect for the park or anywhere you have a bench or chair you can use. Time to level up.

Goal: 3-5 rounds / Time: 20 min / Intensity: Moderate

1. BENCH JUMPS

A - Start in a standing position, squatting to prepare for your jump.
B - Jump off the ground and land on the bench with feet planted firmly and soft knees. Return to start position on ground. That is one rep; do 20.

2. BULGARIAN SPLIT SQUAT (FOOT ON CHAIR)

A - Facing away from the bench, place one foot on the ground and one on the bench behind you in a lunge stance.
B - Lower into a lunge as low as you can go. Make sure chest is tall and front knee doesn't pass the toes. Return to start. That is one rep; do 12 - 15.

3. ELEVATED SIDE LUNGE

A - Stand beside bench and start with right foot on top of the bench. Try to keep hips even.
B - Lower into a side lunge with left foot remaining on bench. Return to standing, leaving left foot on the bench. That is one rep; do 12 - 15 on each side.

4. DECLINE PUSH UP

A - Start in plank position placing hands shoulder width apart with both feet on top of bench.
B - Lower chest to ground, maintaining straight back. Return to starting position. That is one rep; do 12 - 15.

5. DECLINE SHOULDER TAPS

A - Start in plank position with both feet on the bench.
B - Shift weight to left hand and bring right hand up to tap the left shoulder. Then bring the left hand up to tap the right shoulder. Keep the hips as still as possible by engaging core. That is one rep; do 20.

chiselclub.com
photographs and graphic design by Fredy Soberanis (soberanisproductions.com)

CHISEL CLUB WORKOUT: FIELD'S PLAY

This workout is designed for the great outdoors. Find a park or a field where you can sweat in the beauty of nature. There are suggested reps given for each exercise, but if possible, you can also use markers in nature (ie. trees, flowers, benches) to set the distance for these traveling exercies. Happy sweating!

Goal: 3-5 rounds / Time: 20 min / Intensity: High

1. HIGH KNEES
A - Start standing. Drive right knee up towards chest, then lower.
B - Drive opposite knee into chest, switching the legs quickly and at the same time, as if jogging. This is one rep; do 30.

2. WALKING LUNGES
A - Start standing. Step right foot forward and lower into lunge, bring left foot forward and raise into standing position.
B - Step left foot forward and lower into lunge and return to standing. That is one rep; do 15 - 20.

3. CRAB WALK
A - Sit on the floor with knees bent and feet flat on the ground. Lift hips off the ground.
B - Travel forward in this position. Do 20 - 30 reps.

4. PARALLEL DUCK WALK
A - Start in low squat position, thighs are parallel to the ground or lower, torso upright.
B - Stay in the low position and walk forward. Do 20 - 30 reps.

5. BURPEES
A - Stand with feet hip width apart. Jump up off the ground explosively.
B - As you land, bend forward, place hands on the ground and kick feet back into a plank position. Drop chest all the way to the ground, push back up to plank and jump feet into a squat. Return to starting position. That is one rep; do 12 - 15.

chiselclub.com
photographs and graphic design by Fredy Soberanis (soberanisproductions.com)

CHISEL CLUB WORKOUT: OUT OF THE BOX

Why stay in one place when you can move! Take this one outside with some friends and enjoy taking up as much space as possible. Challenge your body as you travel in different directions with these exercises. See which ones challenge you the most and then work on perfecting it.

Goal: 3-5 rounds / Time: 20 min / Intensity: High

1. INCHWORM TO PUSH UP

A - Hinge forward and place hands on the ground with legs straight. Walk hands away from legs and into a plank position.
B - Do a pushup and then walk hands back to feet. Stand up. That is one rep; 20 12 - 15.

2. LATERAL SHUFFLE

A - Start in an athletic stance, knees bent, chest upright and weight on the toes.
B - Shuffle laterally to the right to a designated marker or about 10 steps. Shuffle back to the start. That is one rep; do 10.

3. BROAD JUMPS

A - Begin in squat position with body weight more in the front of the foot. Jump forward as far as you can go.
B - Land in squat position. That is one rep; do 20.

4. BEAR CRAWLS

A - Start on all fours with knees bent and lifted off the ground. Keep knees close to the ground.
B - Crawl forward in this position moving opposite hand and foot at the same time. One crawl forward equals rep. Do 20 - 30 reps.

5. HIGH KNEES

A - Start standing. Drive right knee up towards chest, then lower.
B - Drive opposite knee into chest, switching legs quickly and at the same time, as if jogging. This is one rep; do 30.

chiselclub.com
photographs and graphic design by Fredy Soberanis (soberanisproductions.com)

CHISEL CLUB WORKOUT: PUT IN WORK

If you want to be ready for Summer, or for life in general, you have to put in the work. This circuit is perfect for your busy summer schedule. All you need is a bench or chair so you can do it anywhere. Take it outside to the park, workout at home, in your hotel room or even in the airport during your layover. Get ready, stay ready.

Goal: 3-5 rounds / Time: 25 min / Intensity: High

1. STEP UPS

- **A** - Standing in front of bench, place right foot firmly on top of bench and bend knee at 90 degree angle.
- **B** - Shift weight stepping onto bench and stand tall. Lower left leg back to starting position. That is one rep; do 20 on each side.

2. INCLINE PUSH UPS

- **A** - Facing bench, begin in plank position with hands on bench..
- **B** - Lower chest towards bench, maintaining a straight line from shoulder to ankle, and then press back up into starting plank position. That is one rep; do 15 - 20.

3. DIPS TO TOES TOUCH

- **A** - Face away from bench with feet flat on the ground. Lower into a squat and place hands on edge of bench with fingers facing towards you. Arms are straight, supporting body weight. Bend elbows and lower your body towards the ground.
- **B** - Straighten arms and raise body back up to starting position. Then, extend left arm to touch right foot; repeat toe touch with right arm and left foot. That is one rep; do 20.

4. JUMP BOX SWITCHES

- **A** - Stand facing towards the bench. Place one foot on the bench and the other on the ground.
- **B** - Jump into the air pressing off of both feet. Switch legs in the air so when you land the opposite foot is on the bench. That is one rep; do 40.

5. SINGLE LEG SQUAT TO BENCH

- **A** - Start by facing away from the bench. Stand on your right leg. Left leg is in front of you hovering above the ground.
- **B** - Squat down with control and sit onto bench keeping left foot off the ground. Stand back up using only the right leg, pushing through the heel of the standing leg. That is one rep; do 15 - 20 each side.

chiselclub.com
photographs and graphic design by Fredy Soberanis (soberanisproductions.com)

> There's something sexy about a woman who can do it herself.

DO IT YOURSELF

Nowadays, there seems to be toxic chemicals in just about every store-bought product out there. It can be quite the chore reading the novel of ingredients in your day to day products. I am here to show you how to do it yourself, with real, minimal ingredients to create your own products that are beneficial for you.

It's all about creating healthy habits, so let's start now.

Girl, You Got This.

Here are a 10 of my favorite DIYS.

Bug Spray

Did you know Deet is a known eye irritant and causes rashes, soreness, or blistering when applied to the skin?! DEET also has a negative impact on wildlife and water sources and is toxic to birds and aquatic life. Say NO to Deet.

ESSENTIAL OILS
- CITRONELLA
- CLOVE
- LEMONGRASS
- ROSEMARY
- TEA TREE
- CAJUPUT
- EUCALYPTUS
- CEDAR
- CATNIP
- LAVENDER
- MINT

WITCH HAZEL

DISTILLED WATER

VEGETABLE GLYCERIN OR ALOE GEL [OPTIONAL]

APPLE CIDER VINEGAR [ACV]

Fill 8 oz. spray bottle 1/2 full of distilled or boiled water

Add witch hazel to fill almost to the top bottle

Add 1/2 tsp vegetable glycerin or aloe

Add 4 drops of ACV

Add 30-50 drops of essential oils to desired scent. The more oils used, the stronger the spray will be.

Now get back to enjoying your summer bug free, without harming the environment or your beautiful skin.

Himalayan Salt Deodorant

Did you know antiperspirant prevents the body from purifying toxins which when trapped, find their way into the lymph nodes, where they contribute to cellular changes that could possibly lead to cancer?! Antiperspirant has also been linked to Alzheimer's Disease. If you can, please stay away from the following ingredients: Parabens, Propylene, Glycol, Triclosan, Steaareths. *I got you sister.*

Ingredients

- 3 OZ. DISTILLED WATER
- 2 TSP FINE HIMALAYAN PINK SALT
- 1 OZ. WITCH HAZEL
- 1 TSP BAKING SODA
- 10 DROPS ESSENTIAL OIL OF CHOICE
- SMALL FUNNEL OR MEASURING CUP
- 4 OZ. AMBER GLASS SPRAY BOTTLE

Heat the distilled water until very warm.

Dissolve Himalayan sea salt and baking soda in water. Let water cool completely.

Mix in witch hazel and 10 drops of essential oil. Stir well.

Carefully pour the Himalayan salt deodorant into a glass spray bottle, by using a small funnel or Pyrex measuring cup.

Spray onto clean, dry underarms as needed.

Smell good and feel good naturally!

Chia Pops

Did you know chia seeds are packed with calcium, vitamin c, iron, potassium, and Omega-3? Chia pops are more than just a pretty dessert, they're a total energy boost.

1 3/4 CUPS CANNED COCONUT MILK
3/4 CUP SOY MILK
[OR ANY MILK ALTERNATIVE]
1/4 CUP + 1 TBSP. CHIA SEEDS
1/2 TBSP. AGAVE SYRUP,
OR MORE TO YOUR LIKING
3 KIWIS, PEELED AND SLICED

Stir together coconut milk, soy milk, chia seeds, and agave syrup. If desired, add additional ingredients to sweeten to taste.

Place sliced kiwis in popsicle molds using chopsticks or the back of a spoon to press kiwi to the sides of the mold.

Gently pour liquid mixture into popsicle molds. Insert wooden popsicle sticks.

Freeze for at least 4 hours until popsicles are solid. Enjoy!

To read more about the amazing health benefits chia pops provide, head over to BluHazl.com.

All Natural Bronzer

Do you want that summer glow without the sun damage?
Yup, thought so. Here's a very easy recipe for you to get that bronzed contour, on point, all summer long.

INGREDIENTS

- CORNSTARCH
- COCOA POWDER
- [FOR UNDER TONES OF YELLOW, ADD TURMERIC]

Find a big makeup brush, one you would use for loose bronzer powder and a small 4 oz. mason jar.

Start with 1 tablespoon of cornstarch and slowly add cocoa powder until the shade begins to compliment your skin tone.

NOTE: If you have a more yellow skin tone like me, add a pinch of turmeric for that golden finish.

Test color on a clean part of your arm and add more corn starch or turmeric as needed to adjust shade.

VOILA! Who would have thought you could create the perfect bronzer from ingredients in your pantry! BAM!

Rosewater Spray

Rosewater facial spray is probably one of my favorite beauty essentials! Rosewater has a delicate floral fragrance that offers several beauty benefits for hair, skin and health. Why buy commercial brands when you can just DIY?

INGREDIENTS

4 OZ. DISTILLED WATER
2 OZ. WITCH HAZEL
2 OZ. ROSE WATER
ROSE FLOWERS

To make rose water, remove petals from stems and run them under lukewarm water to remove any leftover residue.

Add petals to a large pot and top with enough
distilled water to just cover the petals [be careful, any more water will dilute the rosewater].

Over medium-low heat, bring the water to a simmer and cover. Let simmer for 20-30 minutes or until petals have lost their color and are a pale pink. Strain the mixture to separate the petals from the water. Here is your rose water.

To create the Rosewater Spray, simply combine witch hazel with rose water and store it in a spray bottle. Shake well before use.

You can use rosewater spray to set your make up, to help with acne, as a body mist, pillow spray, or a hair mist!

Body Wash

Does your body wash ever irritate your skin or leave your skin feeling dry? Well, I've dealt with this issue too many times so I decided to create my own body wash and I have noticed quite a change in the texture of my skin!

INGREDIENTS

- 3 TABLESPOONS LIQUID CASTLE SOAP
- 3 TABLESPOONS RAW HONEY
- 2 TABLESPOONS OILS
- [USE 1 TBSP EACH OF CASTOR OIL AND OLIVE OIL]

Carefully mix all ingredients using a spoon in a glass liquid measuring cup.

[Do not use a blender or whisk, this will create bubbles and make it impossible to transfer into a container]

Pour mixture into a container, preferably glass, and use in the shower as a body wash.

Cheers to smooth and moisturized skin, from your very own body wash creation. Go girl!

Homemade Shampoo

I must admit, I've tried many DIY shampoos and I was never happy with the results. I have finally found a recipe that I'm happy with that doesn't leave my hair tangled, thanks to the hair gods above!

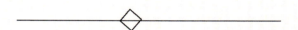

Ingredients

- ¼ CUP COCONUT MILK (HOMEMADE OR CANNED)
- 1/4 CUP LIQUID DR. BRONNER'S CASTILE SOAP
- 10 DROPS LAVENDER ESSENTIAL OIL
- 10 DROPS ROSEMARY ESSENTIAL OIL
- ADD ½ TSP OLIVE OR SWEET ALMOND OIL [OPTIONAL]

Combine all ingredients together in an old shampoo bottle or jar

Shake well to mix ingredients.

Use about a teaspoon every time you shampoo. Shake well before each use and keep in shower for up to a month.

Note: Add Apple Cider Vinegar to the mixture for extra shine!

Apple Cider Vinegar For The Win

Did you know Apple Cider Vinegar can be utilized in so many ways? Apple Cider Vinegar or ACV, along with Coconut Oil are amongst my all-time FAVORITE healing ingredients.

HERE ARE SOME QUICK AVC FACTS:

- ACV is known for kicking that curing Candida, also known as yeast.
- ACV fights Acid reflux
- ACV detoxes the body
- ACV regulates PH
- ACV aids in Weight loss

HERE ARE 5 ESSENTIAL WAYS TO USE APPLE CIDER VINEGAR

1. Drink Up

Drinking two teaspoons of ACV in the morning can help kick start your day! ACV is an incredible detox that helps maintain your body's natural pH, helps promote a healthy liver, and kills Candida.

2. Face Food

ACV is a great toner for the face! It will not only tighten skin but it will also help reduce inflammation and acne. Yes please!

- All you need is 1 part ACV and 2 parts water.
- Add mixture to an empty spray bottle and there it is, your all natural ACV toner!

3. Hair Shine

ACV is the PERFECT Hair rinse!
Mix 1 part ACV with 1 part water.
Use after shampoo!

4. Burn relief

Ever been so sunburned that it hurts to even lay down? ACV to the rescue. Take a bath with 1 cup of ACV in it! It will take the sting right away!

5. Produce Wash

Whenever I go grocery shopping, I wash all my produce right when I get home. I wash everything from apples, spinach, to berries and more. Here is how to make this easy ACV wash: Take 4 tablespoons ACV and 1 gallon of water. Pour mixture into a spray bottle and wash that produce.

For more AVC lovin' head over to BluHazl.com.

Aloe Green Tea Facial Scrub

Did you know humidity can clog pores and create annoying blackheads? No worries, I am going to let you in on one of my favorite blackhead buster facial scrubs.

INGREDIENTS

1/3 CUP COCONUT OIL
1/4 CUP SUGAR
1 TBS. ALOE VERA GEL
2 GREEN TEA BAGS
3-4 DROPS JOJOBA
5-6 DROPS TEA TREE ESSENTIAL OIL
[OPTIONAL, HELPS WITH ACNE]

Cut open tea bags

Add the dry tea to the rest of the ingredients in a bowl and mix.

Scrub onto problem areas. [add or subtract sugar to adjust scrubby vibes, or adjust the coconut oil]

The aloe green tea facial scrub is extremely moisturizing and will leave your face feeling as soft as a baby's bottom. Hello summer nights!

Green Turmeric Lemonade

Would you agree that we all could use an energy boost sometimes?
Here's one of my favorite go to energy drinks
for those early, dreary mornings.

INGREDIENTS

1 LIME
1/2 LEMON
1/2 TSP TURMERIC
1/2 TSP MATCHA
1 TBSP. COCONUT OIL
GROUND BLACK PEPPER TO TASTE
STEVIA

Juice the lime and lemon into a large glass.

Add the matcha and turmeric, along with some freshly ground pepper and combine well.

Fill the glass with cold water, and mix together well.

Add the coconut oil and stir. The oil will separate and float on top, which is OK, don't be alarmed!

You can also use a hand-held blender to help combine them better and make the mixture frothy and smooth (keep in mind, they will eventually separate again). Serve immediately!

To learn more about each significant, key ingredient in this superfood energy drink, head over to BluHazl.com.

—

Remember, we are all a work in progress. We hope that our passions have filled your hearts and inspired you to live a healthier, happier, and stronger lifestyle. Surround yourself with women who push you to be your best self. Never stop improving and working on yourself, because we all need you. Find her, love her, and be good to her. We love the woman that you are becoming.

GIRL, YOU GOT THIS!

BluHazl

BLUHAZL.COM

Made in the USA
Monee, IL
13 September 2020